How to Make Liqueurs

How to Make

LIQUEURS

R.M. Byrne

Kangaroo Press

To my ever willing band of tasters,
without whom this work would not have
been possible

Photography by Dale Meyer

First published in 1991 by Kangaroo Press Pty Ltd
3 Whitehall Road (P.O. Box 75) Kenthurst NSW 2156
Typeset by G. T. Setters Pty Limited
Printed in Singapore by Kyodo Printing Co (S'pore) Pte Ltd

ISBN 0 86417 384 9

Contents

Introduction

Just when, where and by whom the first liqueurs were made has been lost in the vapours of time. What we do know, however, is that the forerunners of liqueurs as we know them today were around as far back as 400 years before the birth of Christ.

In more recent times, the liqueur has been associated with the wealthy, to be partaken of in an atmosphere of intimacy, in good company and reserved for very special occasions. Today, with the advent of simple methods for making the liqueurs at home, more and more people are becoming aware of their pleasurable significance and the use of liqueurs in entertaining, social events and the quiet evening at home alone is an every-day occurrence.

This book is a guide to making your own liqueurs. It provides recipes suitable for the 'home brewer', as well as different ways to use the liqueur you create, such as in delicious desserts and chocolates.

It also explains the terms used in the preparation and making of liqueurs.

The need for this book has become obvious from the response I have received from all around Australia for copies of recipes which were published in the *Sunday Telegraph* (in NSW), and I am indebted to the *Sunday Telegraph* personnel for making it possible for me to expand the original collection of recipes and information to what has been presented here.

Making liqueurs is perhaps the newest home craft to be undertaken in recent years, and those who have dabbled in 'making their own' have found it not too time-consuming, with the reward of the lasting pleasure and satisfaction that comes from using one's imagination to create a fine (and unique) product.

To make the liqueurs in this book you won't need complicated equipment; just scales, containers, a filter and a selection of ingredients most of which can be found in your home and garden, or in the local supermarket. However, it is essential that you understand that every liqueur has an alcohol base. The alcohol may seem to be expensive at first glance, but when you compare the results of your finished product—the quantity of liqueur you have produced—with the cost of commercially produced liqueurs, you will see that there is a great difference in the cost in your favour; and you have the added pleasure of having created, with a little experimenting, a product more suitable to your individual taste.

May you discover the pleasure that results from having created your own liqueurs, and may you experiment as I have, to find new and interesting ways of using your finished products.

Types of Liqueurs

Following are the types of drinks usually classified as liqueurs. Liqueurs are sweetened spirits, usually flavoured with a selection of flowers, spices, fruits, herbs, nuts, berries, etc. with an alcohol content of at least 22%, but more usually around 35%.

Ratafia

This is usually the name given to liqueurs prepared from fruit juices; but sometimes it is used for liqueurs made from flowers, where the ingredients have been allowed to stand for some time, rather than being distilled.

Bitters

This refers to a variety of liqueurs flavoured with certain bitter herbs and spices. They may be sweetened or unsweetened. Unlike other liqueurs (which are drunk *after* meals), bitters are usually drunk as an aperitif; either straight or (if very concentrated, such as angostura bitters) added in a few drops to other drinks.

Elixir

This is a drink which is said to improve health and life expectancy. An unsweetened elixir, however, does not qualify as a liqueur.

For centuries, liqueurs have been created to honour famous people or events in history; in the same way, organisations would often give instructions for the production of their own liqueur. An example of this originated in 1834 with the production of Bols 'freemasons liqueur' for the centenary of the Dutch Lodge.

Women were often immortalised by having their names given to certain liqueurs—Eau de la belle Agathe being perhaps the most well known of these.

During earlier times, liqueurs were stronger and much spicier, and the alcoholic content was around 50%.

Variations on Liqueurs

During my research I discovered a number of rather strange concoctions which people have tried to pass off in the name of 'liqueur'. Some were claimed to have miraculous properties, but the contents alone would cause you to look elsewhere for your 'miraculous' cure! Spiders' heads, animal testicles and chicken droppings were among the most absurd ingredients.

But be assured, although there are some unusual recipes included in this book, few of them include ingredients that cannot be found in most homes or supermarkets. The exceptions are those recipes included for fun and for interest's sake.

Medicinal Liqueurs

For centuries people have turned to distilled alcohol for medicinal purposes; during the Middle Ages brandy was only sold as a medicine and taken in minute quantities.

During the many epidemics which flourished during the 14th century (for example the Black Death, 1340–1350), people paid big money for a few drops of this precious liquid, and physicians were quick to recommend brandy because of the feeling of wellbeing it gave—if not an actual cure!

Brandy has been credited with curing the common cold, headaches, lethargy, and my mother swears by it for mouth ulcers. It is said to have cured baldness and killed lice and fleas. A few pieces of cotton wool soaked in brandy, squeezed out and put in the ears, together with drinking a little at bedtime, is said to have cured deafness. It is good for toothache and sweetens the breath, can cure shortness of breath and make a poor speaker eloquent! It is said to be good for the digestion and appetite and for removing wind from the body. For a clear memory and courage, brandy taken in moderation is the answer. Whether or not brandy does induce such cures is up to the reader to determine, but it must certainly make the suffering much more bearable!

It was during the Middle Ages that people started adding spices and herbs to their brandy, and spared no expense in the preparation of their 'remedies', probably thinking that 'the costlier, the better' would apply. When you look at the recipes which finally evolved from these early experiments, you can perhaps see that the combinations of herbs and spices used would have some curative effects rather than the alcohol in which they were steeped.

Love Potions

Herbs have a long history of having a love-stimulating effect, in certain combinations. In the Middle East some fantastic love potions have been concocted using alcohol to increase the effect, and sweetened to make them more palatable.

When taken in large amounts some herbs do, indeed, appear to arouse passionate feelings, and in the Middle Ages sorceresses or the so called 'white witches' believed in the power of such love potions. However, there were also the 'black witches' whose potions were used for more evil purposes.

Love potions, along with the witches who brewed them, have long since lost their appeal and have all but disappeared from present day society. However, for the adventurous among you, some recipes have been included for you to try containing such herbs as dill, cinnamon, cardamom, caraway, coriander, nutmeg and celery; all of which are believed to be aphrodisiacs.

Fruits in Liqueur

One of today's most exotic luxuries must surely be 'Fruits in Liqueur'. These fruits look magnificent in attractive containers, soaking in the most delicate of the liqueurs. Once you have made your liqueur, you may like to try the recipes for 'Fruits in Liqueur' and see the reaction when you give these as gifts.

Desserts and Chocolates

With the growing popularity of liqueurs, some interesting and delicious recipes have been devised using the liqueur as a flavouring base. In these sections you will find some recipes to try using the liqueurs you have made.

About the Ingredients

Alcohol

The alcoholic base used in your liqueurs depends on your own preferences as well as the ingredients you intend using. Each class of distilled drinks has a taste and smell all its own, and this can vary from product to product.

When you consider all the different brands of whisky, brandy, rum and gin, the variations to the flavour of your end products are endless, and you can achieve some extremely subtle tastes by experimenting with the various brands of alcohol.

Sweetening

The most commonly used sweetening agent is plain sugar. Some of the older recipes recommend the use of sugar-candy because it imparts a more pleasant flavour, but today the difference is of little importance. Loaf-sugar is sometimes used, as is honey, which gives a completely different taste. Occasionally it is required to boil the sugar into a syrup with water and cool before using, which ensures that the sugar is well-dissolved before it is added to the drink, but this has the disadvantage of diluting the liquid and weakening the taste. It is preferable not to add the sugar to the alcohol at the same time as the spices, herbs, fruits, etc., as sugar inhibits these from secreting their flavours and aromas. Instructions about sweetening will accompany each recipe.

Fruits

It is important that the fruit you use is fresh, ripe (but not over-ripe), wiped well to remove debris and traces of sprays and free from any sign of pest infestation. Unsprayed fruits are the best to use, but are not always readily available. Fruit that has to be washed must be dried well to prevent the liqueur from becoming watery.

Rinds

Rind cut from citrus fruits should not have any pith attached, so should be peeled very carefully.

Berries and Flowers

These should be wiped carefully if there is any sign of debris.

Herbs and Spices

The herbs used may be either fresh or dried. Dried herbs should be good quality with much of the original aroma still present. Avoid old or musty herbs and spices. Seeds and roots, etc. may be crushed to obtain the best extracts, but these can also be ground in a coffee-mill or food processor if more convenient.

Most of the herbs and spices used in these recipes can be found in your local supermarket, health food shop, or even in your garden. For a few of the more exotic ones, however, you may need to try a specialist outlet, such as an Asian supermarket or a herbalist.

Nuts

When using nuts in making liqueurs the shells may or may not be used, according to the recipe. Shells should be wiped before cracking to ensure that they are clean. Liqueurs made from nuts usually have some sediment which will escape the filtering process, so you will have to decant the liquid to ensure that it is crystal clear.

Colouring

Your liqueur will look more attractive if certain colourings are used, but these will not change the taste. Most liqueurs develop an excellent colour from the ingredients used, but if the colour does need improvement, simply add a few drops of tasteless and odourless edible dye until you have attained the colour you want. Substituting brown sugar for part of the sugar content, for example, will result in an attractive brown colour.

Measures

The recipes give both metric and the equivalent Imperial quantities. Please note that these conversions are approximate only.

The quantities given are intended as a guide only, and may be adjusted to suit personal tastes.

Liqueur Making Methods

The distinctive quality of each liqueur is attained from the combination of aromatic ingredients which flavour the alcohol, rather than from the alcohol itself. These characteristics are formed in a number of different ways.

Distilling

This is the method by which the ingredients, such as spices, roots and rinds are steeped with a fermentation product for a few days, using gentle heat. The liquid is then converted into vapour by heating and cooling. This process had to be repeated many times in days gone by to attain a high level of alcohol, but with modern day equipment, one operation can result in a level of 96%.

Because it is illegal to own a still in so many areas, this method will not be used for the recipes in this book. In his book *On Drink*, Kinsley Amis cites a joke (perhaps based on fact), to demonstrate how easy it is to be charged if found in possession of a still:

A man was accused of distilling without a licence and was brought to court.

'Where is the proof of this charge?' roared the judge.

'This was found on his premises,' answered the prosecutor as he displayed what was, undeniably, a condenser.

'Case proven,' said the judge. 'Does the accused have anything to add?'

'Yes, your honour. I would therefore also like to plead guilty to rape!'

'You would like to do what?' exclaimed the surprised judge as he eyed his elderly defendant. 'Why do you say that?'

'If it please your honour, although I have the equipment for both charges, I am not capable of using either!'

Digesting

In a closed boiler, under controlled pressure, the ingredients are steeped in alcohol at around 70°C. This method is mainly reserved for the production of bitters.

Macerating

This is the method mostly used for the recipes in this book. It consists of soaking the ingredients in the alcohol for a given period of time so that the alcohol becomes imbued with the taste and aroma of the plants, fruits, spices, etc. used.

Each recipe will indicate the amount of time the ingredients are to be soaked in the alcohol. Don't worry if you are unable to adhere to these times precisely—it is a recommendation only, and depends on factors such as weather conditions, number of ingredients and the position in which the macerating process is taking place. As some plants do not yield their aromatic components by some of the other methods, this is the method usually employed to ensure that resins, fats, acids and proteins are retained by the alcohol.

Percolating

As in coffee making, the flavour and aroma of, for example, coffee or cocoa beans is captured by this method, which allows the alcohol to trickle slowly through a thick layer of the ground beans—with or without heating.

Explanation of Terms Used

Position

Opinions differ about the position in which a liqueur should be stored during the extraction period. Some recommend a cool dark position and others a warm light position. Herbs macerate well in a moderately warm position, but some of the softer fruits are better if left for a longer time in a cool position. Extracts kept in a handy position will enable you to give them a shake from time to time, which is important in some recipes to achieve good results.

Filtering

Filtering your liqueur is most important, as the liqueur should be crystal-clear. A strong paper filter will do the job quite well; however a nylon filter, or even a thoroughly sterilised finely woven handkerchief, will allow you to squeeze out the last drops of the liquid without danger of sediment escaping into the drink.

Decanting

If there is still sediment in the liqueur after you have filtered it, then you will need to decant the liquid.

Allow the sediment to sink to the bottom of the container then carefully pour the liquid into another bottle, ensuring that the dregs are not allowed to escape.

Aqua-vitae

This term is used when referring to the alcohol to be used in a particular liqueur. It is an un-rectified alcohol: brandy is perhaps the best example.

Christmas Cheer (page 27)

Creme de Menthe (page 30)

Chocolate Strawberry Flan (page 63)

Blackberry Liqueur (page 24)

Cherry Vodka (page 27)

Cherry Liqueur (page 25)

Cherries in Cherry Liqueur (page 59)

Eau de vie

Another term referring to the alcohol content of the liqueur. Although brandy will suffice, a better result will be achieved from a light French brandy, although many people prefer to use a clear alcohol, such as vodka, if a white eau de vie is unavailable.

Rectified Alcohol

This is pure alcohol and not readily available to the general public in this country. Should a recipe call for 'rectified alcohol' then you should use a product with a high proof rating. 96% is about as high as I have found.

Helpful Information

Sterilising

All utensils, bottles, filters, etc. must be thoroughly cleansed before use and free from any trace of taste or odour from previous contents. Items should be rinsed in soap-free water so that the danger of contamination from soap is avoided. If in doubt about your utensils and containers, soak in soda water for half an hour, scrub with a clean brush if necessary, rinse, and dry by standing upside-down. Soak corks in boiling water for about 10 minutes then dry completely before using. The containers in which your liqueur is to macerate should be quite air-tight to prevent evaporation of the alcohol.

Maturing

Most liqueurs require time to mature so that the aroma and flavour can develop to their full potential. The longer the better is usually a good rule, and after a few years (if you can resist temptation that long) a more fragrant and rounder flavour will have developed. Fruits in alcohol are an exception as some fruits are too soft and unpleasant to eat at the end of their maturing time.

Storing

Once you have bottled and sealed your liqueur, it should be kept in a cool, dark place until required. Some, such as those containing milk products and eggs, are best stored in the refrigerator, and have a limited life span. The others will keep for quite a long time once opened, if you remember to seal well after each use.

Making Adjustments

When making liqueurs it is important to remember that, with only very slight adjustments, better results can be obtained. Taste is all important, and most of the world-famous liqueurs were developed through a constant adjustment to taste.

The order in which ingredients are placed into the mixing bottle is of some importance and a better result is usual if the alcohol is added last. Do not worry if your container is not full, or that you leave a half-empty bottle for any length of time. As liqueurs are high in both alcohol and sugar content, they produce an environment in which bacteria cannot survive.

Do not be concerned about the strength of your drinks—if it tastes right, then it is right! If it does not seem strong enough, gradually add a little more alcohol until a satisfactory taste has been achieved. If it is not sweet enough, stir in a little more sugar. Naturally, if you do not like the taste of certain alcohols, for example gin, do not use this as a base for your liqueur.

When substituting an alcohol base, take care to replace a clear base with a clear substitute; likewise, you should replace a coloured base with a coloured substitute.

Presentation

Having made your own special liqueurs, you will be anxious to share them with your friends, and as gifts, liqueurs that you have made yourself are very acceptable. It is important, therefore, that you bottle the liqueur in attractive containers. Some sauce, cordial and mayonnaise bottles, for example, are excellent for this purpose, and as long as the bottles have been thoroughly cleansed, with no trace of odour from the previous contents, make attractive presentation size containers. The bottles should be labelled and attractively wrapped. Ensure that they are well sealed. For your own use, too, presentation is equally as important. The bottles in which your alcohol was purchased are sometimes quite attractive, and can be used for storing or serving your liqueur. For special occasions use an attractive decanter for serving.

The Liqueurs

Almond Liqueur

250 g (½ lb) sweet almonds
1 teaspoon cinnamon
1 teaspoon cloves
5 teaspoons bitter orange rind
350 g (12 oz) sugar
1 litre (32 fl oz) brandy

Chop the almonds and add to the remaining ingredients, except sugar. Put into a container with the brandy, seal well and allow to stand for 1 month, shaking from time to time, then filter and add sugar. Bottle and seal.

Shake once a day until sugar has dissolved, and leave for 2 months before using.

Angostura-style Bitters

(This recipe is included mainly for interest's sake, as some of the more exotic ingredients, such as tonka beans, may be difficult to obtain.)

2½ teaspoons gentian root
2½ teaspoons galangal root
2½ teaspoons angostura bark
3½ teaspoons cardamom

3½ teaspoons cinnamon
½ teaspoon angelica
½ teaspoon ginger root
4 cloves
3½ teaspoons orange rind (bitter)
17 g (½ oz) sandalwood
17 g (½ oz) tonka (also called tonquin) beans
1 litre (32 fl oz) brandy
50 g (2 oz) sugar

Soak the herbs, spices and rind in the alcohol for 14 days in a sealed container in a moderately warm position.

After this extraction period, filter and add sugar, stirring well until dissolved, then bottle and seal well. Leave 6 months in a cool, dark position before opening.

Apricot Brandy

1 kg (2 lb) fresh apricots
a little white wine
500 g (1 lb) sugar
1 litre (32 fl oz) brandy

Pierce apricots a few times with a silver fork. Bring a saucepan of water to the boil and add the apricots. Allow to simmer for about 2 minutes. Strain off the boiling water and run cold water over the fruit. Let stand in this water for 10 minutes, then drain. Peel the apricots, halve them and remove stones. Crack the stones and take out the kernels.

Make a syrup with the sugar and some white wine; to this add the apricots and kernels. Bring to the boil again, then sieve out the apricots and kernels with a straining spoon and put them aside in a preserving jar. Discard kernels. Allow the syrup to simmer until it thickens. Cool and pour over the apricots. Add the brandy and close the jar tightly. Allow 2 months before opening.

Bishop's Essence

30 g (1 oz) orange rind (bitter)
3 cloves
1 stick cinnamon
1 ½ teaspoons nutmeg
1 ½ teaspoons ginger root
1 ½ teaspoons cardamom
1 litre (32 fl oz) brandy

Combine all ingredients and allow to soak for at least 3 weeks. Filter and bottle. Seal well. When required, add one tablespoonful to a bottle of red wine with sugar, to taste; warm slightly and serve.
    (Very economical for gift giving.)

Blackberry Liqueur

500 g (1 lb) blackberries
200 g (7 oz) sugar
a piece of lemon rind
750 ml (16 fl oz) preserving brandy

Clean the berries thoroughly and place in a preserving jar. Sprinkle the sugar on top and add the lemon rind and some allspice (optional). Pour the brandy over the berries and close the jar tightly. Shake carefully from time to time. Leave for at least 2 weeks; but better still, leave to mature for a month, then filter and bottle.

Brandy Alexander Liqueur

400 g (10 oz) sweetened condensed milk
225 g (7½ oz) reduced cream
1 cup brandy
3 teaspoons vanilla essence

In a blender, combine all the ingredients and blend until smooth.
Transfer to a storage container, seal well and chill until required.
Makes about 3½ cups.

Chartreuse (Imitation)

¼ teaspoon saffron
13 whole cardamoms
rind of 2 lemons
400 g (13 oz) sugar
1 litre (32 fl oz) brandy

Remove seeds from cardamoms and allow all the ingredients to soak
in the brandy for 4–6 weeks in a sealed container. Keep in a
moderately warm position.
After the extraction period, filter and add the sugar.
Bottle and allow to mature for 6 months in a cool, dark position.

Cherry Liqueur

500 g (1 lb) red cherries
3 cups vodka

1 cup water
500 g (1 lb) caster sugar

Thoroughly wash, stem and pit the cherries. Place cherries in a securely covered container with the vodka and water and let stand for 7–10 days; until liquid is a deep red colour.

Strain and discard cherries.

Add the sugar, stirring well until completely dissolved, then let stand overnight before bottling. Seal well.

Cherry Liqueur (Dry)

1 kg dark, late, sour cherries
3 × 50 g (2 oz) portions of castor sugar
1 cup pre-boiled warm water (20°C)
4 cups Pure Polish Spirits

Wash cherries and remove stems. Place cherries in a large bottle with one 50 g portion of castor sugar. Mix well and add warm water. Seal well with a cork and tape cork securely in position. Leave in a cool, dark place for 24 hours. Then add the second portion of castor sugar and stand for another 48 hours. After this period, add the final portion of sugar and stand for a further 48 hours. This fermentation should take a total of 5 days. The fruit should be kept in a dark position throughout. After the last period, add the spirits to the fruit and set aside for 36 hours.

Next, pour all the liquid (fruit juice and spirits) into a second bottle, cork securely and set aside for 6 weeks to clarify in a cold, dark position.

Filter carefully and pour into bottles.

Note: The cherries can be reserved and used to make a lighter liqueur.

Cherry Liqueur (Sweet)

1 kg (2 lb) dark, late sour
  cherries
3 × 150 g (5 oz) portions of
  sugar

1 cup warm water, pre-boiled
4 cups Pure Polish Spirits
  (96% proof)

Prepare the same way as for Dry Cherry Liqueur.

Note: The cherries can be reserved and used for Cherry Vodka.

Cherry Vodka

Use the reserved cherries from either of the above recipes.

100g (3 oz) castor sugar
1 cup Pure Polish Spirits
1½ cups water

Add sugar to the cherries and place in a large jar. Mix well by shaking
the jar after being well sealed.

Set aside in a cool, dark position for 7 days. Strain the juice which
has formed and mix with the Polish Spirits and water.

Filter well and pour into clean bottles. Cork well, and keep in
a cool, dark place for at least 30 days before using.

Christmas Cheer Liqueur

400 g (13 oz) sweetened
  condensed milk

225 g (7½ oz) reduced cream
1½ cups whisky

1 egg   2 teaspoons strong black coffee
1 tablespoon chocolate dessert
  topping

Put all the ingredients into a blender and combine well until smooth.

Transfer to storage container, seal well and refrigerate until required. Makes about 3½ cups.

Note: quantities may be adjusted to suit individual tastes in this and other recipes.

Coffee Liqueur

60 g (2 oz) ground coffee
1 little vanilla and/or cocoa
1 litre (32 fl oz) eau de vie or brandy
250 g (½ lb) sugar

Allow the ingredients to soak in the alcohol (except the sugar) for at least 4-6 weeks, in a bottle that can be closed securely. Place in a moderately warm position.

After extraction, filter and add sugar, stirring well until completely dissolved.

Bottle, seal and if possible, leave to mature for another 6 months or so in a cool, dark position.

Compote of Fruits in Liqueur

Fill a large jar with a variety of summer fruits: peaches (and peach stones), blackcurrants, strawberries, raspberries, mulberries, cherries, etc.

Top up with brandy or vodka and add 6 cloves, a cinnamon stick and sugar to taste.

Seal well and allow to stand until winter before opening.

Filter and bottle.

Cream of Rum Liqueur

1 tin (400 g, or 13 oz)
   sweetened condensed milk
½ cup rum
600 ml (1 pint) cream
2 tablespoons chocolate
   topping

2 teaspoons coffee powder
2 teaspoons hot water
½ teaspoon ground cinnamon
½ teaspoon vanilla essence

Place all ingredients into a blender and blend well. Pour into sterilised bottles, seal well.

Label and store in refrigerator for 2 weeks before using.

This liqueur may be frozen. Makes about 3 cups.

Creme de Cacao

30 g (1 oz) cocoa
½ teaspoon vanilla
piece of lemon rind

1 litre (32 fl oz) vodka
450 g (15 oz) sugar

Allow all ingredients (except sugar) to soak in the alcohol for 5–6 weeks in a securely closed bottle in a warm place.

After this extraction period, filter and add sugar, stirring well until dissolved. Bottle and allow to mature for 6 months or so in a cool, dark position.

Creme de Menthe (White)

3 cups vodka
1 cup water
75 g (2 ½ oz) peppermint essence (white)
2 cups caster sugar

Mix vodka, water and mint essence well and cover securely. Let stand for 10 days then strain and add sugar. Shake carefully until sugar has dissolved. Cover and let stand overnight, then bottle and seal.

Creme de Menthe (Green)

¾ cup sugar
1 cup water
1 ¼ cups gin
½ teaspoon peppermint essence (green)

½ teaspoon green food colouring
½ cup washed, green mint leaves

Boil sugar and water, stirring continuously until sugar has dissolved completely. When cold, add remaining ingredients and stand overnight. Remove mint leaves and filter if required before bottling. Seal well.

Cumquat Liqueur

1 kg (2 lb) ripe cumquats
3 cups vodka

1 cup water
2 cups caster sugar

6 whole cloves   1 teaspoon ground cinnamon
2 tablespoons whole coriander
  seeds

Wash fruit well and cut into quarters lengthwise. Discard seeds. Cover the fruit with the vodka, water, cloves, coriander and cinnamon.

Seal container well and leave for 21 days, then strain through a large sieve. Add sugar and stir until dissolved. Pour mixture into a tall bottle and allow to clear; this takes about 7 days.

Decant carefully into clean bottles and discard residue.

Cumquat Liqueur No. 2

500 g cumquats
2 cups sugar
1½ cups brandy

Wash fruit well, then prick all over with a darning needle. Combine cumquats, sugar and brandy in a large sterilised jar with a plastic lid. Seal and turn jar every day for 4 weeks until the sugar has dissolved.

Strain liquid into a sterilised bottle for storage. Seal and label. Store in a cool dark place. Makes about 3 cups.

Curacao (Blue)

1 teaspoon cinnamon   400 g (13 oz) sugar
15 g (½ oz) mace   blue colouring
1 litre (32 fl oz) vodka   a little almond essence

Place all the ingredients (except the sugar and colouring) into a well sealed container and allow to stand for 4–6 weeks in a moderately warm position.

Filter and stir in the sugar. Add the colouring. Pour into containers and store for 6 months in a cool dark position before opening.

Curacao *(Orange)*

Toast the rinds of 3 oranges until a light brown. When cool, put into a container with a litre of rum and allow to soak for 6 weeks.

Make a syrup of 350 g (¾ lb) sugar and a little water and add the rinds of 3 fresh oranges. Simmer for 3–4 minutes. Cool. Pour into the rum mixture and leave to soak for 6 weeks in a sealed container, then filter and bottle.

A little mace and a few cloves and/or cinnamon may be added, if liked, before standing for 6 weeks.

Drambuie

4 cups Scotch whisky
2 cups orange honey (from
  health food stores)

3½ tablespoons whole
  coriander seeds

Combine all ingredients and shake vigorously until all the honey has dissolved completely. Cover container securely and seal. Leave to mature for 28 days.

After 28 days, strain through a fine sieve, filter and bottle in dark-coloured bottles.

Note: because the quality and flavour of the honey will vary from region to region, you may have to experiment to get this recipe to suit your particular taste.

Dutch Bride's Tears

500 g (1 lb) seedless raisins
200 g (7 oz) almonds
1 cinnamon stick
sugar-candy to taste
1 litre (32 fl oz) brandy

Place raisins into a preserving jar. Blanch the almonds, peel and chop them up. Add the almonds to the raisins along with the cinnamon stick, sugar and brandy. Seal the jar and let stand for 2 weeks. Filter and bottle.

Variation: add a piece of lemon or orange rind and a few cloves. Dutch gin may be used instead of brandy.

Grand Marnier

4 cups vodka
4 oranges—juice and skin
3 cups caster sugar
1 tablespoon coriander seed

75 g (2½ oz) imitation
    brandy essence
Brown food dye (*see* Note)

Wash and peel oranges. Separate pith from the skin and discard the pith. Squeeze oranges and strain well. Using a large mixing jar, place the juice, skin, vodka and coriander seeds inside, cover securely and leave in a warm, dark place for 14 days. Strain through a coarse sieve and discard residue. Return juice to jar and add brandy flavouring and sugar. Shake well until all sugar has dissolved. Let stand until clear—at least 14 days.

Decant and add brown colouring (if using) mixed with a little of the liqueur. Liqueur should be a very pale brown colour. Seal well and store until required.

Note: Instead of using dye, you can substitute 1 cup of brown sugar for 1 cup of the caster sugar.

Grapefruit Liqueur

2 grapefruit
rind of ½ orange
10 sweet almonds
1 bottle whisky

Wash and dry grapefruit well. Cut off several thin slices of rind and put into a preserving jar. Cut the fruit into segments and remove the membranes between them. Place in the jar with the orange rind and chopped almonds.

Pour the whisky over, seal well, then leave for 4 weeks. Strain and filter the liqueur and if required, sweeten with sugar to taste.

Note: remaining grapefruit segments may be added to fruit salad or to seafood.

Hangman's Orange Liqueur

¾ cup sugar
1¾ cups brandy
1 large orange, unpeeled
2 large buttons

1 wide-necked jar with screw-top plastic lid (approx. 1 L, or 32 fl oz)
20 cm (50 in) fine string

Hangman's Orange (page 34)

Liqueured Chocolate/Nuts (pages 75-6)

Orange Chocolate Sherbert (page 76)

Peach Ratafia (page 42)

Curacao – Blue & Orange (pages 31–2)

Rose of Turin (page 48)

Dutch Bride's Tears (page 33)

Irish Cream Flan (page 67)

Place sugar into sterilised jar. Pour in the brandy. *Do not stir.*

Pierce a hole in the middle of the lid with a heated skewer. Thread through the string and secure to the top of the lid with one button. Thread other end of string through the orange. Secure at bottom of orange with the other button. Adjust when screwing on lid so that the orange is suspended above the brandy when lid is securely in place. Orange *must not* come into contact with brandy.

Rotate orange 360° by twisting the button on the lid every day for 2 weeks. Remove orange. Stir sugar into the brandy until dissolved.

Pour into attractive, sterilised bottles. Seal and label. Decorate for gift giving.

Note: a very tasty liqueur—and one in which you can see the extraction process at work.

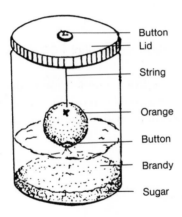

Highland Bitters

25 g (1 oz) gentian root	1 cinnamon stick
3½ teaspoons bitter orange rind	3 teaspoons cloves
15 g (½ oz) coriander seeds	1 litre (32 fl oz) whisky
½ cup chamomile flowers	sugar to taste (optional)

Allow the spices and herbs to soak in the whisky for 4–6 weeks. Make sure that the container is well sealed and in a moderately warm position.

After extraction, filter the liquid and stir in the sugar if using, then bottle, seal and allow to mature for 6 months before use.

Honey Liqueur

10 g (⅓ oz) peppermint herb
1¼ teaspoons thyme
1¼ teaspoons hyssop
1 litre (32 fl oz) rum
250 g (½ lb) honey

Allow the herbs to soak in the alcohol for a week, then filter and add honey.

Bottle, seal and shake from time to time to dissolve the honey. *Note:* different brands of alcohol can produce a variation of flavours in this liqueur. Experiment to find the one that suits you best.

Irish Cream Liqueur

1 tin (375 ml, or 12 fl oz)
    evaporated milk
1 tin (400 g, or 13 oz)
    condensed milk
20 drops vanilla

1 tablespoon drinking
    chocolate (*not* cocoa)
300 ml (10 fl oz) whisky
6 eggs

Combine all ingredients in a large bowl and beat well. Bottle, seal and refrigerate.

Note: Irish cream liqueur must be drunk fairly soon, as it will not keep indefinitely (about 4–6 weeks).

Lavender Liqueur

150 g (5 oz) lavender flowers
3 teaspoons aniseed
3 teaspoons peppercorns
1 litre (32 fl oz) brandy
350 g (¾ lb) sugar

Put flowers, herbs and brandy into a preserving jar or bottle and seal. Allow to stand for 6 weeks.

Filter and add sugar, stirring until completely dissolved. Bottle and seal.

Lemon Liqueur

rind of 4 lemons
rind of 1 orange
a few bruised coriander seeds
1 clove
400 g (13 oz) sugar
1 litre (32 fl oz) eau de vie or
  vodka

Place rind, coriander and clove in a bottle and pour over the alcohol. Cover securely and leave for 1 month.

Filter the liquid and add sugar, stirring until dissolved. Seal jar and leave a few weeks before opening.

Variations: substitute cinnamon, mace and orange blossom for the clove and coriander.

Mint Liqueur

100 g (3 oz) mint leaves
100 g (3 oz) peppered spirit of mint
½ cup orange blossom
1 litre (32 fl oz) brandy
350 g (¾ lb) sugar

Soak all the ingredients, except sugar, in the brandy in a well-sealed container for 4–6 weeks. Stand in a moderately warm position.

After extraction, filter and stir in the sugar, then bottle and leave in a cool dark place for 6 months before opening.

Morello Ratafia

1 kilo (2 lb) morellos (dark red cherries)
5 teaspoons mace
1 clove
½ cinnamon stick
100 g (3 oz) sugar
1 litre (32 fl oz) brandy

Crush morellos, pips and all. Add the spices and cover completely with brandy.

Close container securely and allow to soak for 4 weeks. Filter and add sugar. Shake from time to time until the sugar has dissolved.

Allow to stand for 2 months before using, but it is better if left until the tree is in bloom again.

Mulberry Liqueur

500 ml (16 fl oz) mulberry purée
piece of cinnamon stick
4 cloves
piece of vanilla pod
piece of lemon rind
300 g (10 oz) sugar
1 litre (32 fl oz) eau de vie

Place all the ingredients (except the sugar) into a jar and let stand to macerate for 6 weeks.

Filter and add sugar—check taste as you go. Allow to stand for 6 weeks before using.

Orange Coffee Liqueur

1 very large orange
44 coffee beans
44 lumps sugar
½ vanilla pod
1 bottle Cognac or eau de vie

Use the best, largest orange you can find, with a thin rind and unsprayed (if possible). Wash well, rub dry, and with a knife make as many small cuts in the orange as possible.

Stick the coffee beans into these cuts, and put any that are left over in the bottom of a preserving bottle. Put the orange with its 'bodice' of beans into the bottle with the 44 lumps of sugar. Add the vanilla pod, then the Cognac.

Allow to mature for 44 days, then filter and bottle. Seal well and store until required.

Parfait Amour

1½ teaspoons coriander
½ teaspoon cinnamon
½ teaspoon mace
4 cloves
1½ teaspoons iris powder
  (white flag/violet root)

2 teaspoons bitter almonds
piece of lemon rind
1 litre (32 fl oz) eau de vie
  (vodka)
500 g (1 lb) sugar

Allow the herbs and spices to soak in the alcohol for 4–6 weeks in a securely closed container. Stand in a moderately warm position.

After the extraction period, filter and stir in the sugar.

This liqueur is improved if coloured; amethyst being the most suitable. This colour is achieved by mixing a little red and blue colouring together.

Peach Ratafia

750 g (1½ lb) peaches
pinch of cinnamon
pinch of cloves
pinch of nutmeg
sugar to taste
1 bottle vodka

Cut peaches, skin and all, into small pieces; crack the stones and chop up the kernels. Put the flesh, kernels, cracked stones and spices into a preserving jar, cover with a cloth and leave mixture to soak for a few days. You can pour the vodka over immediately, as long as you seal the jar. Allow to stand for a month.

Strain through a linen filter and squeeze out well. Add sugar to taste and stir until dissolved. Filter. Allow to stand for a few months after bottling before opening for particularly delicious liqueur.

Pears in Brandy

quantity of pears
juice and rind of 1 lemon
piece of cinnamon stick
brown sugar to taste
brandy

Peel pears, remove cores and cut into pieces. Make a thick syrup with half the weight of the pears in sugar and a little water. Add the pear pieces, bring to the boil and simmer gently for 5 minutes.
   Allow to cool, then filter.
   Cover generously with rum, bottle and seal well.

Note: this drink will not keep indefinitely.

Pear Liqueur

6 fresh or 12 dried pears
3 cups vodka
1 cup water
1 orange
6 whole cloves

1 teaspoon whole coriander
   seeds
1 teaspoon ground cinnamon
3 whole peppercorns (optional)
4 cups caster sugar

If using fresh pears, wash, seed, stem and dice; if using dried pears, roughly dice.
   Place diced pears in a jar with herbs and spices. Cut zest off the orange, leaving behind the pith. Peel orange, discard pith, break into segments and cut into halves. Place orange zest and segments in a jar with water and vodka. Cover well and leave in a dark place for 14 days.
   Strain through a coarse sieve, then strain through a medium sieve, and finally strain through a fine sieve. Add caster sugar and shake well until dissolved.

Leave to clear in a cool, dark position for seven to ten days.

Decant carefully into a clean bottle and discard any dregs. To improve colour, add a little yellow food dye.

Peppermint Liqueur

25 g (1 oz) peppermint herb
4 cloves
½ teaspoon mace
a handful of orange blossom

20 g (⅔ oz) lemon rind
1 litre (32 fl oz) brandy
250 g (½ lb) sugar

Allow the herbs, spices, rind and blossom to soak in the brandy for 4–6 weeks in a well sealed bottle. Stand in a moderately warm position.

After extraction, stir in the sugar, filter and bottle.

Note: this liqueur may need a little green colouring to enhance its appearance.

Persico

250 g (½ lb) peach stones
50 g (2 oz) almonds
rind of 1 lemon
4 cloves

piece of cinnamon stick
1 litre (32 fl oz) brandy
sugar to taste

Crack peach stones and remove kernels. Chop kernels and almonds and put them into a jar together with the cracked stones, lemon rind, herbs and spices. Pour the brandy over, seal well and let stand for 6 weeks. Shake occasionally and add the sugar.

When the sugar has dissolved filter, bottle and leave for 6 weeks before opening.

Pineapple Liqueur

1 medium sized ripe
  pineapple
500 g (1 lb) caster sugar
½ teaspoon whole coriander
  seed
½ teaspoon ground cinnamon
3 cups vodka
1 cup water

Skin and dice pineapple and place in a jar with coriander, cinnamon, vodka and water. Cover well and leave in a dark place for 14 days, then strain well through a fine sieve and save pineapple for future use.

Add sugar and shake until dissolved.

Allow to clear (this takes 7–10 days), then decant carefully into clean bottles. Seal well and store until required.

Note: the soaked pineapple can be added to fruit salad or fruit cake for an interesting flavour.

Prince of Orange Liqueur

40 g (1 oz) apricot stones
3 teaspoons orange blossom
2 teaspoons angelica seed
2 teaspoons angelica root
2½ teaspoons cinnamon
⅓ teaspoon vanilla essence
350 g (12 oz) sugar
1 litre (32 fl oz) brandy

Place alcohol and herbs into a well sealed container and soak for 6 weeks in a warm position.

After this extraction period, filter and stir in the sugar until dissolved.

Bottle and seal. Leave in a cool dark place for 6 months before opening.

Pumpkin Liqueur

750 g (1½ lb) pumpkin
juice and rind of 1 lemon
750 ml (25 fl oz) rum

175 g (6 oz) sugar for each
500 ml (16 fl oz) of juice

Cut pumpkin into small pieces, add the juice and rind of the lemon and bring to the boil. Simmer until pumpkin is soft. Rub through a sieve and add the rum and sugar.

Cover well and let stand for 1 week, then filter carefully and bottle.

Raspberry Liqueur

500 g (1 lb) raspberries
300 g (10 oz) sugar
pinch of ground cinnamon
1 litre (32 fl oz) Kirsch

Check fruit for blemishes and discard any with marks. Carefully wipe berries and place in a jar. Sprinkle the sugar over the berries and add the herbs last. Pour over the Kirsch then seal the bottle.

Allow 1 month to macerate, then filter. Pour into storage bottles and seal well. Allow to mature for 3 months before using.

Raspberry Ratafia

500 g (1 lb) raspberries
250 g (½ lb) cherries
350 g (¾ lb) sugar

1 litre (32 fl oz) eau de vie
(vodka or brandy)

Carefully crush the washed cherries (fruit and pips) with a pestle and add the raspberries, which should be squashed a little. Pour over the alcohol and leave to soak for 2 weeks in a tightly closed jar.

Squeeze the pulp through a linen filter to get as much juice as possible, and add the sugar.

Leave for 14 days, then filter and bottle. Do not open too soon.

Rockmelon Liqueur

6 large ripe rockmelons
3 cups vodka
1 cup water
2 cups caster sugar

2 teaspoons whole coriander seed
6 whole cloves

Quarter the melons, remove and discard seeds and skin. Place melon quarters in a container with cloves, coriander, vodka and water. Cover securely and leave in a warm, dark place for 14 days.

Filter and bottle, adding sugar and shaking well until dissolved. Leave 7–10 days to clear and decant if necessary. Tint with orange food dye if a better colour is required.

Rose Bouquet

50 g (2 oz) crown petals of a
  heavily scented rose
25 g (1 oz) currants
3 level teaspoons jasmine
  flowers

¼ teaspoon cinnamon
¼ teaspoon mace
3 cloves
750 ml (24 fl oz) brandy
200 g (7 oz) sugar

Combine all ingredients (except the sugar) and pour into a bottle. Seal well and allow to stand 1 month.

Filter and add sugar, stirring until dissolved. Allow a few weeks before opening.

Rose of Turin

60 g (2 oz) sweet smelling roses
50 g (2 oz) jasmine flowers
50 g (2 oz) orange blossom
10 g (⅓ oz) cinnamon

1½ teaspoons cloves
2 teaspoons mace
a piece of lemon rind
1 litre (32 fl oz) brandy
sugar

Place all the ingredients in a preserving jar and seal well.
Allow to stand for 1 month, then filter and add sugar to taste.

Note: this liqueur can be given a nice purple colour to enhance its appearance.

Strawberry Ratafia

500 g (1 lb) sweet strawberries
300 g (10 oz) raspberries
400 g (14 oz) sugar

vanilla
a few coriander seeds
1 litre (32 fl oz) eau de vie

Make a syrup of the sugar with some water by bringing to the boil and leaving to simmer for 5 minutes. Aromatise with the vanilla and coriander.
Pour the hot syrup over the fruit which has been wiped but not washed. Leave the pulp for 4 hours, well covered.
Sieve the pulp and mix with the eau de vie (brandy or vodka),

then filter and bottle. The liqueur may be used in a short period of time.

Note: the pulp can be used for jam-making.

Strawberry Sauterne Liqueur

500 ml (16 fl oz) mashed
    strawberries or strawberry
    purée
1 bottle Sauterne

300 ml (½ pint) rectified
    spirit (*see* Explanation of
    Terms, p.16)
sugar to taste
a piece of lemon rind
    (optional)

Allow all the ingredients (except the sugar) to stand in a sealed container for 2 weeks, then filter and add sugar to taste.
    Do not use for another 2–3 weeks.

Note: instead of Sauterne another sweet white wine may be used.

Tia Maria

1 cup sugar
1 cup hot water
4 heaped teaspoons instant coffee
1 dessertspoon vanilla
1 cup underproof rum

Dissolve sugar and coffee in hot water, then add vanilla. Allow to cool and add rum.
    Bottle, seal, and allow 1 week before opening.

Tomato Liqueur

750 g (1½ lb) tomatoes
½ teaspoon caraway seed
1 teaspoon cloves
1 cinnamon stick
1 bottle vodka
sugar to taste

Using nice firm tomatoes, skin them and cut the flesh into small pieces. Place the pieces into a preserving jar, add the herbs and pour in the vodka.

Seal the jar and stand for 14 days, then filter and add sugar to taste. Bottle and allow to stand 1 month before serving.

Walnut Liqueur

10 fresh, moist walnuts with shells
a piece of cinnamon stick
10 cloves
honey
1 litre (32 fl oz) brandy

Crack the nuts and put them, shells and all, into the alcohol with the cinnamon and cloves. Leave to soak for a month, then filter the liquid, add honey to taste, and leave to mature in well sealed bottles for 2 or 3 months before using.

Note: the nuts may be used afterwards in chocolates—either moulded, or just make clusters.

Zucchini Liqueur

750 g (1½ lb) zucchini
juice and rind of 1 lemon
750 ml (24 fl oz) rum
175 g (6 oz) sugar for each 500 ml (16 fl oz) of juice

Cut zucchini into small pieces and place in saucepan. Add the lemon juice and rind and bring to the boil. Simmer until zucchini has been cooked. Cool and rub through a sieve.

Place into a preserving jar with the rum and sugar and allow to soak for 1 week, then filter well and bottle.

Medicinal Liqueurs and Elixirs

Brou de Noix

12 fresh soft nuts   250 g (½ lb) sugar
10 cloves   1 litre (32 fl oz) eau de vie
1 whole nutmeg   (vodka or brandy)

Pound the nuts finely and put them in a preserving jar. Add the
spices and pour over the alcohol. Leave to soak for 6 weeks.

Sieve the drink through a cloth and squeeze out all the liquid.
Add the sugar and allow to stand for another few weeks in a sealed
container. Filter well and also decant for best results, as sediment
is usually formed.

Note: this drink is good for the stomach; a few teaspoons daily is
all that is required.

Carnation Elixir

Fill a preserving jar with small red carnation petals.

Top up with brandy, a few cloves, a piece of cinnamon stick
(small) and a little mace. Cover the jar securely and allow to stand
for 6 weeks. Filter and add sugar to taste. Leave for another 3 weeks,
shaking now and again to dissolve the sugar.

Note: the French recommend this liqueur for indigestion.

Pineapple Liqueur (page 45)

Raspberry Ratafia (page 46)

Rose Bouquet (page 47)

Walnut Liqueur (page 50)

Peppermint Liqueur (page 44)

French Quince Liqueur

When making quince jam, wash the quinces well and rub dry, then peel.

Peel from above quinces
eau de vie (light French brandy)
350 g (¾ lb) sugar

Place the peel into a preserving jar and cover with the brandy. Allow to macerate for 6 weeks. Filter and stir in sugar. Dissolve well, bottle and seal.

Note: this liqueur is excellent for stomach upsets, according to French tradition.

Rose Hip Liqueur

400 g (13 oz) rose hips
rind of 1 orange
piece of cinnamon stick

1 litre (32 fl oz) vodka
sugar to taste

Cut the rose hips into small pieces and bruise well. Place in a bottle with the herbs and alcohol and stand for 6 weeks. Keep the container securely closed, and shake occasionally.
   Filter and stir in sugar, then bottle.

Note: the fruit that remains after bottling this liqueur can be boiled, rubbed through a sieve, and made into a jelly.
   Rose Hip Liqueur is good for older people—relieving some of their varied illnesses of the 'waterworks' by strengthening and stimulating.

Love Potions

Farmer's Love Potion

4 teaspoons fennel seed
3 teaspoons celery seed
3 teaspoons angelica
2½ teaspoons coriander seed
1 litre (32 fl oz) brandy
sugar to taste

Crush or grind the herbs, then allow them to soak in the brandy
for 14 days. Filter the liquid and add sugar to taste. Stir well until
dissolved.

Just like the farmer's love—this drink needs time to blossom!

Older Man's Love Drops

(This recipe is given just for fun!)

When the moon is full, soak 300 g (10 oz) chopped fresh truffles
in 2 litres (64 fl oz) rum. Leave for 3 days.

Boil 12 crayfish for 20 minutes in a boiler with thyme, caraway,
pepper, anise, cinnamon, nutmeg and 1 stalk celery, chopped. Rub
through a sieve to produce a soft purée, then thicken by stirring
over a gentle heat.

Press through a cloth filter and add finely chopped liver from
a 2 year old white chicken. Allow to macerate 3 hours, then add

rum and 1 litre of 80% proof brandy. Cover well and allow to soak overnight.

Sieve and filter, then add 3 teaspoons angelica and stand for 1¼ hours before bottling.

A glass for thee...
The old man too...
And the flush of young love
Will return to you!

Magic Charm

20 g (⅔ oz) cinnamon
½ cup scented rose petals
¼ cup nutmeg
1 litre (32 fl oz) eau de vie
sugar candy to taste

Place spices, rose petals and eau de vie in a bottle, seal and allow to soak for 14 days, then filter well and add sugar candy.

Bottle and seal well, and allow to mature for 2–3 months for the flavour (and magic!) to develop.

Fruits in Liqueur

Apricots in Liqueur

300 g (10 oz) dried apricots
sugar to taste
rind of 1 lemon
1 cinnamon stick
250 ml (8 fl oz) water
1 litre (32 fl oz) brandy

Place apricots and water in a preserving jar, seal and let stand for 24 hours. Transfer to a saucepan, add sugar, lemon rind and cinnamon stick and bring to the boil. Simmer for 10 minutes, then cool.

Put apricots with the syrup into an attractive container then add the brandy. Seal well and allow to stand for 3 months before opening.

Brandied Cherries

Cut cherries from the tree leaving on a little of the stalk (or choose cherries with stalks when buying). Wash well and dry. Half fill a decorative bottle, then spoon in some sugar and shake until cherries are coated. Add more cherries and sugar as above. Pour in brandy, cover and let stand overnight. Top up bottle with brandy and seal well.

Best if left for 2 years! However, cherries can be tested after a few months and eaten if well flavoured with the brandy. When the cherries have been eaten, you may then drink the cherry brandy.

Figs in Brandy

500 g dried figs
1 ½ cups water
½ cup brandy
¼ cup brown sugar firmly packed
1 lemon

Place figs, water and brandy in a large saucepan and bring to the boil slowly. Cover and reduce heat. Simmer for about 30 minutes until tender. Stir in sugar and the lemon peel which has been cut into thin strips. Simmer for 5 minutes. Add the juice of the lemon and combine well, then pour into clean, warm jars and seal. Store in a cool dry place. Will keep for about 12 months.

Fruits in Pre-made Liqueurs

Fruits in Liqueur using some of the softer fruits, are possible using pre-made, matured liqueurs. These will not keep as long as the other fruits in liqueur, but are still an exotic taste sensation and welcome gift.

Orange Wedges in Liqueur

Peel and remove all pith from oranges. Carefully quarter segments and add to any orange or orange/coffee flavoured liqueur. Seal and allow to stand for a week or so, for the flavour to penetrate the orange pieces.

Pears in Liqueur

Peel and core firm pears. Slice into 6 segments lengthwise and add to pear flavoured liqueur.

Pineapple in Liqueur

Peel fresh pineapple and cut into wedges, or use tinned pineapple. Put into pineapple flavoured liqueur and allow to stand until the flavour has penetrated the fruit before using.

Combinations of fruit and compatible liqueurs may be used, but don't use a liqueur with a strong taste as this will overpower the flavour of the fruit.

Plums in Liqueur

750 g (1 ½ lb) plums
piece of cinnamon stick
piece of lemon rind
350 g (¾ lb) sugar
750 ml (25 fl oz) brandy

Wash the plums and dry them well. Wtih a darning needle, prick them here and there right through to the stone. Make a syrup by bringing the sugar, cinnamon stick and rind to the boil in a little water. Keep just off the boil for 5 minutes, then allow to cool.

After 24 hours, remove the plums from the syrup, put them into a jar and reboil the syrup until it thickens. When cool, pour over the plums and add the brandy.

Make sure the jar is well sealed and store for a few months before opening.

Prunes in Port

750 g (1½ lb) dessert prunes, stones removed
3 cups port
¼ cup brown sugar
2 cinnamon sticks
rinds of 1 orange and 1 lemon cut into strips

Place prunes in bowl and heat remaining ingredients together in a saucepan until boiling point is reached. Pour over prunes and allow to cool completely. Remove cinnamon sticks. Place prunes in a jar and pour the syrup over until completely covered.

Seal tightly and allow 1 week before using. Will keep for about 12 months.

Liqueur-based Desserts

Brandy Alexander Ice-cream

3 egg yolks
½ cup sugar
1 tablespoon plain flour
1 cup milk
½ cup cream
1 tablespoon creme de cacao
1 tablespoon brandy
½ cup cream (extra)

Whisk egg yolks, sugar and flour together until pale and thick. Place milk and cream in a small saucepan and bring to the boil, but do not allow to boil. Whisk milk mixture into egg mixture and return to saucepan. Cook, stirring constantly, until mixture coats the back of a metal spoon. Stir in remaining ingredients. Pour into swiss roll tin. Freeze. Serve with brandy snaps. Serves 8.

Note: any coffee flavoured liqueur may be used in place of creme de cacao.

Chocolate Roll (Spicy)

200 g melting chocolate
200 g almonds (ground)
200 g sugar

15 g slivered almonds
15 g mixed peel, chopped
1 teaspoon Tia Maria
grated rind of ½ lemon
juice of ½ lemon
1 teaspoon cinnamon
1 large egg
extra sugar

Place all ingredients, except egg and extra sugar, into a saucepan and stir over low heat until melted. Remove from heat and quickly mix in egg. Cook for 1 minute, stirring constantly.

Sprinkle 2 sheets of greaseproof paper with the extra sugar and place half the mixture on each. Form into a roll about 3 cm in diameter. Wrap in the paper and refrigerate. To serve, cut into slices.

Will keep for up to 3 months.

Chocolate Strawberry Flan

Base

125 g (4 oz) plain chocolate biscuits
90 g (3 oz) butter or margarine
1 tablespoon sugar

Filling

90 g (3 oz) dark chocolate
3 eggs (separated)
1½ tablespoons Tia Maria
1 tablespoon cocoa
3 teaspoons gelatine

1½ tablespoons water
½ cup cream
1 tablespoon sugar

Topping

1 punnet large strawberries
13 g (½ oz) pkt red cake glaze (Cake Glaze is available in
    13 g (½ oz) packets at most supermarkets and large food
    stores.)

Base

Combine finely crushed biscuits, sugar and melted butter in a bowl
and mix well. Press mixture into a well greased springform pan.
Refrigerate until ready to use.

Filling

Place chopped chocolate in top of double saucepan and stand over
simmering water until chocolate has melted. Remove from heat
and cool 1 minute. Stir in egg yolks, one at a time. Combine cocoa
with Tia Maria and stir into mixture. Whip cream and sugar
together until soft peaks form, then fold into the chocolate mixture.
Sprinkle gelatine over water, stand over hot water until gelatine
has dissolved. Stir dissolved gelatine into chocolate mixture; whip
egg whites until soft peaks form and fold into chocolate mixture.
Pour mixture into prepared base and refrigerate until firm.

Topping

Wash and hull strawberries, slice thinly. Arrange sliced strawberries
over top of filling. Prepare glaze according to directions on packet,
using 1 cup of water and 2 tablespoons sugar. Spoon glaze over
the strawberries and refrigerate until required.

Creme de Cacao Cheesecake

Base

60 g (2 oz) butter
60 g (2 oz) dark chocolate

90 g (3 oz) plain sweet
   biscuits, crushed
60 g (2 oz) ground hazelnuts

Filling

250 g (½ lb) cottage cheese,
   sieved
250 g packet cream cheese,
   softened
½ cup sugar
1 teaspoon vanilla essence
2 teaspoons gelatine

2 tablespoons hot water
225 g (7 oz) tin reduced
   cream
2 egg whites
2 tablespoons brandy
2 tablespoons creme de cacao

Topping

2 teaspoons gelatine
2 tablespoons hot water
225 g (7 oz) tin reduced
   cream
1 tablespoon brandy

1 tablespoon creme de cacao
2 teaspoons sugar
1 teaspoon instant coffee
   powder
nutmeg to decorate

Base

In a small saucepan, melt together butter and chocolate over low heat, stirring until smooth. In a bowl combine biscuit crumbs and nuts. Add butter mixture and stir until combined. Press mixture into greased, foil-lined lamington tin. Chill.

Filling

In a bowl, beat together cottage and cream cheeses until smooth. Gradually beat in sugar and vanilla. Dissolve gelatine in hot water and beat into cheese mixture with the reduced cream. Beat egg whites with clean beaters until stiff then fold into mixture with creme de cacao and brandy. Pour into prepared base and chill until set.

Topping

Dissolve gelatine in the hot water. In a bowl, combine reduced cream, brandy, creme de cacao, sugar and coffee powder. Add gelatine and whisk together until well combined. Spread over filling and sprinkle nutmeg on top. Chill until required.

Fruity Marnier Tartlets

1¼ cups flour
¼ cup icing sugar
⅓ cup margarine
1 egg yolk
2 tablespoons water
1 cup milk
1 vanilla bean
2 tablespoons cornflour
2 egg yolks (extra)

⅓ cup unsalted butter
⅓ cup icing sugar (extra)
1 tablespoon Grand Marnier
strawberries, washed and
    hulled
kiwi fruit or fruit in season,
    sliced
glace cherries, quartered

Sift flour and icing sugar. Rub in margarine. Add egg yolk and sufficient water to make a stiff dough. Knead lightly. Chill. Roll pastry out thinly between 2 sheets of greaseproof paper.

Cut using a 6 cm (approx. 2½ in) fluted cutter. Line 2 sets of greased shallow patty tins. Prick. Cut 48 small holly shapes from remaining pastry and place on greased scone tray. Bake pastry cases

in oven at 190°C (375°F) for 20 minutes. Bake holly leaves at 190°
(375°F) for 5 minutes. Allow to cool. Bring milk and vanilla bean
to the boil. Simmer 3 minutes. Cool slightly. Remove bean.

Blend cornflour and extra egg yolks with milk. Heat, stirring
constantly until thickened. Chill. Cream butter and extra icing
sugar. Add the custard and liqueur. Beat well and chill. Place a
piece of fruit on the base of prepared pastry cases. Pipe creme
patisserie over fruit using a rose pipe. Decorate with holly leaves
and cherries.

Icy Citrus Bowl

4 large oranges
3 grapefruit
2 tablespoons sugar
2 tablespoons Curacao (or any orange flavoured liqueur)
sprigs of fresh mint

Peel oranges and grapefruit. Remove all pith and cut into segments.
Place in a large bowl. Sprinkle fruit with the sugar and liqueur.
Cover and chill for 2 hours before serving.

Serve in individual dishes garnished with fresh mint leaves.

Irish Cream Flan

Flan base

125 g (4 oz) shortbread   ½ teaspoon cinnamon
   biscuits   60 g (2 oz) butter or
½ cup coconut   margarine

Filling

125 g (4 oz) packet cream
  cheese
1 tablespoon honey
1 tablespoon sugar
2 eggs (separated)

½ cup Irish Cream
2 teaspoons gelatine
2½ tablespoons water
300 ml (10 fl oz) carton
  cream

Coffee Cream Topping

2 teaspoons instant coffee
  powder
¼ teaspoon cinnamon

1 tablespoon water
30 g (1 oz) dark chocolate

Flan

Crush biscuits finely and put coconut into a heavy based pan. Stir
with wooden spoon over moderate heat until golden brown. Remove
from heat immediately and add to crumbs with cinnamon and
melted butter; mix well. Press crumb mixture into the base and
sides of a well greased 23 cm (9 in) flan tin. Place into refrigerator
while preparing filling.

Filling

Beat cream cheese, honey and sugar until smooth. Add egg yolks
one at a time, beating well after each addition. Add Irish Cream
and continue to beat well. Sprinkle gelatine over water, dissolve
over hot water, then cool. Add to cream mixture. Beat until
combined. Beat ½ cup cream into soft peaks and fold into cream
cheese mixture, reserving remaining cream for topping. Beat egg
whites until soft peaks form and fold into cream mixture. Pour into
the prepared flan base and refrigerate until set.

  Pipe decorative edge around border of flan with Coffee Cream
topping and spinkle with grated chocolate.

Coffee Cream Topping

Dissolve coffee and cinnamon in water. Put into a bowl with reserved cream. Beat until firm peaks form.

Passionfruit & Mango Mousse

3 teaspoons gelatine
2 tablespoons water
½ cup passionfruit pulp
1 ½ cups fresh or canned mango pulp
3 tablespoons creme de cacao
300 ml (1 ¼ cups) cream

Dissolve gelatine in water over a low heat. Cool then stir in passionfruit and mango pulps. Place over ice until starting to thicken, then stir in creme de cacao. Fold in whipped cream and pour into attractive glass bowl. Decorate with whipped cream, strawberries and passionfruit pulp.

Serves up to 10.

Strawberry Citrus Mousse

1 ½ cups caster sugar
½ cup water
4 egg whites
375 g (¾ lb) strawberries
1 ½ cups thickened cream

Marnier Sauce

250 g (½ lb) strawberries (quartered)
1 teaspoon lemon juice
½ cup Grand Marnier (or orange juice)
1 teaspoon icing sugar

Line 14 cm × 21 cm (approx. 6 in × 8 in) loaf tin with foil. Combine sugar and water in a pan, stir over moderate heat until dissolved, without boiling. Then bring to boil and boil without stirring until syrup reaches hard-ball stage (120°C, or 250°F on sugar thermometer), or when a drop of mixture forms a hard ball when placed in a glass of water.

Beat egg whites until soft peaks form. With beater working, pour syrup into egg whites in a thin stream, continue to beat until the meringue cools completely. (About 20 mins.) Blend strawberries and fold into meringue mixture. Beat cream in a bowl until soft peaks form then fold into meringue mixture.

Pour into prepared pan, cover and freeze for several hours—or overnight. Serve slices of frozen mousse with citrus sauce.

Marnier Sauce

Combine all ingredients in a pan and bring to the boil, then simmer for 7 minutes. Cool slightly and blend mixture until smooth. Push mixture through a sieve to remove seeds.

Tia Maria Cream

4 egg yolks
2 tablespoons caster sugar
3 tablespoons Tia Maria
1 teaspoon brandy (optional)

Tia Maria (page 49)

Strawberry Citrus Mousse (page 69)

150 ml (5 oz) thickened cream, whipped *or* use stiffly beaten
   egg
whites (4) if desired

Whisk egg yolks and sugar together until light and fluffy. Stir in
Tia Maria and brandy. Place bowl over gently simmering water
and whisk continuously until mixture is thick. Cool slightly, then
fold cream through egg mixture and spoon into individual serving
dishes.

Chill well before serving with a strawberry decoration on top.

Chocolates and Other Sweets

Chocolate Kisses

2 egg yolks
⅔ cup icing sugar, sifted
125 g (4 oz) butter or margarine
250 g (8 oz) dark chocolate
2 teaspoons coffee powder
2 teaspoons hot water
2 teaspoons Tia Maria

Place egg yolks and icing sugar in the top of a double saucepan. Heat, stirring constantly, until thickened (about 2 minutes). Cool. Cream butter in a bowl, then beat in egg mixture. Melt the chocolate in the top of a double saucepan. Cool. Beat chocolate into creamed mixture with the remaining ingredients. Refrigerate for 5 minutes. Using a piping bag with a star nozzle, pipe small rosettes into small foil patty cases. Refrigerate. Store in airtight containers. Will keep several weeks. Makes 50.

Chocolate Truffles

90 g (3 oz) butter or margarine
½ cup thickened cream
300 g (10 oz) dark chocolate pieces
2 tablespoons any liqueur or brandy
cocoa

Place butter and cream into a small saucepan. Heat until butter has melted and mixture is boiling. Add chocolate and stir over low heat until melted. Cool for 2 minutes, then stir in liqueur. Transfer to bowl. Cool in refrigerator, stirring occasionally. When firm enough to handle, form teaspoons of mixture into uneven balls.

Sift some cocoa onto grease-proof paper. Roll each truffle in this until generously coated. Refrigerate until firm. Store in an airtight container.

Truffles will keep about 2 weeks in the refrigerator and 6 weeks if frozen.

Note: Tia Maria is an excellent liqueur to use; coconut may be used instead of the cocoa to coat the truffles.

Liqueured Nuts

Take reserved nuts from any nut liqueur, or soak a quantity of nuts in a liqueur for 2–3 days. I used walnuts reserved from Walnut Liqueur and almonds soaked in the Hangman's Orange Liqueur.

Follow directions for melting and moulding chocolate and place a nut, or piece of nut, into the centre with a little of the liqueur. For best results, use dark chocolate for the walnuts and milk chocolate for the almonds.

If walnuts have been retained unbroken, these pieces can be dipped in the chocolate for an interesting result.

If using small pieces of nuts, stir these into the chocolate and form clusters.

Liqueur-filled Chocolates

Follow directions for melting and moulding chocolates.

Make a soft liqueur filling by flavouring a soft icing with liqueur instead of milk.

To make a firm filling, use a liqueur (such as Irish Cream liqueur) to work the icing to the required consistency.

You can vary the liqueur used to suit your taste.

Use white chocolate for a very delicate result; mould and fill chocolates in the usual way.

For the adventurous, chocolates can be filled with the liqueur itself. Take care that chocolates are well sealed to prevent liqueur escaping.

Orange Chocolate Sherbert

6 medium sized oranges
¾ cup caster sugar
juice of 1 lemon
1 tablespoon gelatine
1 tablespoon any orange flavoured liqueur
1 egg white
100 g (3 oz) melting chocolate
2 teaspoons butter or margarine

Cut a thin slice from the top of each orange. Using a spoon, remove the pulp taking care not to damage the skins. Sieve pulp. Add sugar and stir to dissolve. (Do not use heat.)

Sprinkle gelatine over lemon juice and heat gently until dissolved. Cool and whisk into orange juice with the liqueur. If necessary, add water to bring quantity to 3¼ cups. Pour into shallow trays and freeze for 2 hours. Beat egg white until stiff. Whip frozen sherbert until smooth then fold in egg white. Pile mixture into orange peel shells. Freeze 4–5 hours, or overnight.

Before serving, melt chocolate and butter in double saucepan, stirring until smooth. Trickle over orange sherberts and chill for a few minutes before serving.

Truffle Treats

⅓ cup cream
200 g (3 oz) chopped dark chocolate
1 cup biscuit crumbs
2 teaspoons creme de cacao
2 teaspoons Grand Marnier
2 teaspoons any coffee liqueur
1 tablespoon drinking chocolate
2 tablespoons coconut
¼ cup finely chopped pecan nuts

Bring cream to the boil and remove from heat. Add chocolate and stir until melted, then add biscuit crumbs. Chill until firm. Divide mixture into 3 equal portions. Add creme de cacao to 1 portion, Grand Marnier to 1 portion and coffee liqueur to 1 portion.

Roll teaspoonsful of each mixture into balls. Roll creme de cacao balls in drinking chocolate, Grand Marnier balls in coconut and coffee balls in pecans. Chill until firm; serve with coffee.

Index